allargando molto _ _ _ _ _ _ _ _ _ a tempo ♩ = 90

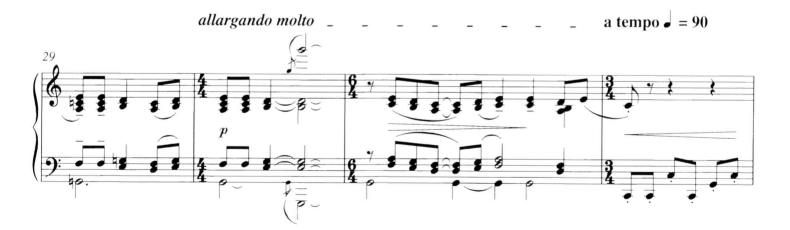

SIMPLE SKETCHES

for Piano
by
NORMAN DELLO JOIO

EXCLUSIVELY DISTRIBUTED BY

HAL•LEONARD®

to my Barbara

SIMPLE SKETCHES

for Piano

NORMAN DELLO JOIO

I.

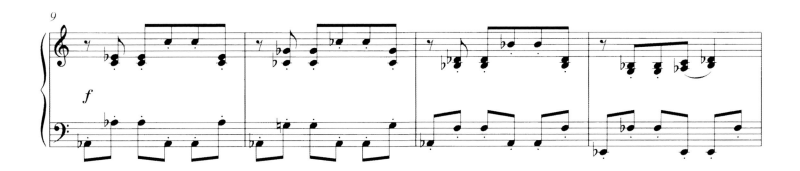

rallentando

Adagio ♩ = 60

Tempo Primo ♩ = 90

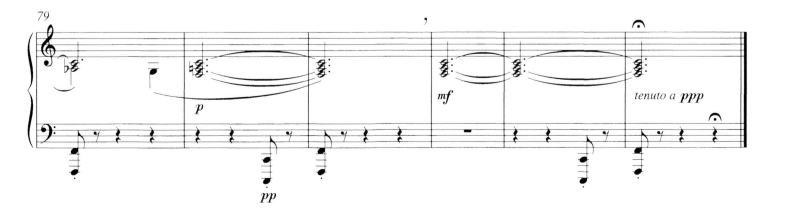

II.

Andante ♪ = 100

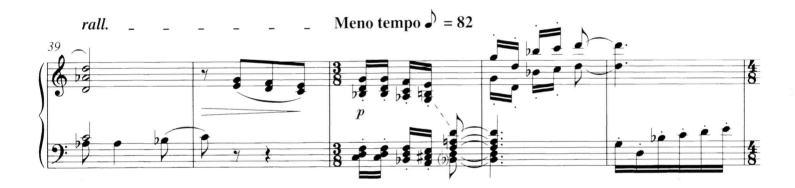

8

un poco rallentando _ _ _ _ _ _ _ Adagio ♪ = 70

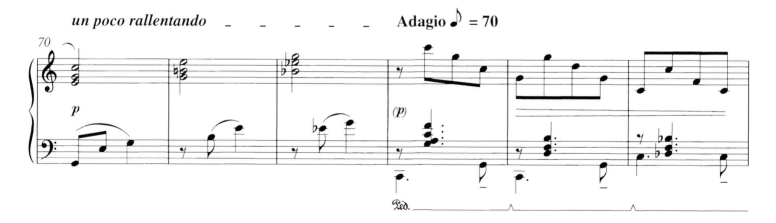

III.

Allegro spiritoso ♩. = 82

Meno tempo ♩. = 60

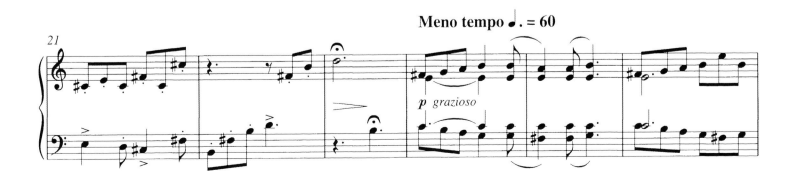

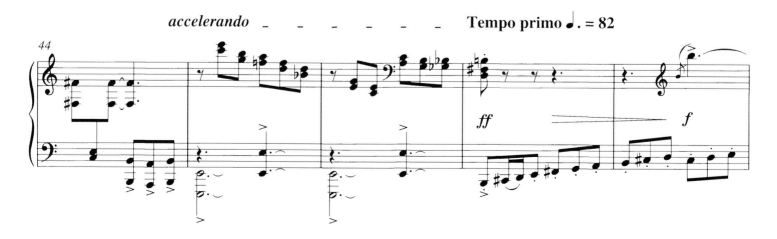

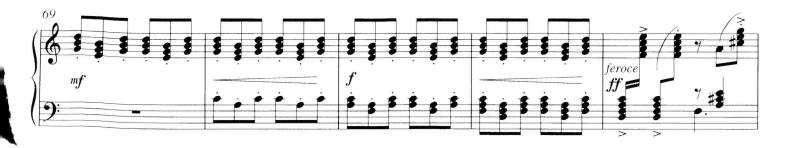

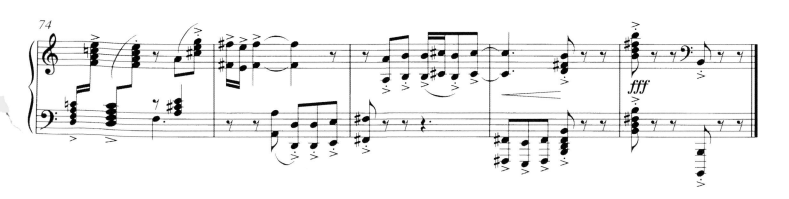

U.S. $8.99

HL00220031

Exclusively Distributed By

HAL•LEONARD®

ISBN-13: 978-0-634-02752-9

Distributed By

HAL LEONARD

00220031